Prefixes & Suffixes
GRADE 3

Editor
Eric Migliaccio

Managing Editor
Ina Massler Levin, M.A.

Cover Artist
Barb Lorseyedi

Illustrator
Sue Fullam

Art Production Manager
Kevin Barnes

Imaging
Rosa C. See

Publisher
Mary D. Smith, M.S. Ed.

Author

Debra J. Housel, M.S. Ed.

Teacher Created Resources, Inc.
6421 Industry Way
Westminster, CA 92683
www.teachercreated.com
ISBN: 978-1-4206-8607-4
©2006 Teacher Created Resources, Inc.
Reprinted, 2013
Made in U.S.A.

Table of Contents

Introduction

The old adage "practice makes perfect" can apply to your child and his or her education. The more practice and exposure your child has with concepts being taught in school, the more success he or she is likely to find. For many parents, knowing how to help their children may be frustrating because the resources may not be readily available. As a parent, it is also hard to know where to focus your efforts so that the extra practice your child receives at home supports what he or she is learning in school.

A child's ability to comprehend what he or she reads depends upon the ability to understand the meaning of new words when they are encountered. A knowledge of prefixes and suffixes helps your student to quickly grasp the meaning of unknown words. This knowledge also serves an important role in expanding a student's vocabulary and spelling abilities. *Practice Makes Perfect: Prefixes and Suffixes* covers the prefixes and suffixes most frequently used in words found in both fiction and nonfiction text. A chart on page 45 shows the meanings of all of the prefixes and suffixes covered.

The exercises included in this book meet or reinforce educational standards and objectives similar to the ones required by your state and school district for third-graders:

- The student will recognize and know the meaning of common prefixes and suffixes.

- The student will use a knowledge of prefixes and suffixes to decode unknown words.

- The student will use a knowledge of prefixes and suffixes to determine the meaning of new words.

- The student will use a knowledge of prefixes and suffixes in order to spell words correctly.

How to Make the Most of This Book

Here are some ideas for making the best use of this book:

- Set aside a specific place in your home to work on this book. Keep the necessary materials on hand.

- Determine a specific time of day to work on these practice pages to establish consistency. Look for times in your day or week that are conducive to practicing skills.

- Keep all practice sessions with your child positive and constructive. If your child becomes frustrated or tense, set aside the book and look for another time to practice.

- The lessons do not have to be done in order. You may choose the lessons that that you feel will be most beneficial to your child.

- Allow the child to use whatever writing instrument he or she prefers.

- Review and praise the work your child has done.

- Assist the student in understanding directions and decoding sentences.

- Promote good test-taking skills on every page by telling your child, "Skip those that you can't figure out and return to them once you've done the others."

- Encourage the child to point out words with prefixes or suffixes in the materials he or she reads.

The Prefix *un-*

When the prefix *un-* starts a word, it means "not."

Examples: *unsaid* means "not said"

unbroken means "not broken"

Part I: Form words by adding *un* to the base word. Write the word on the line.

Example: not hurried _____ unhurried _____

1. not used _____

2. not tied _____

3. not happy _____

4. not certain _____

5. not spoken _____

6. not usual _____

7. not known _____

8. not able _____

9. not do _____

10. not cover _____

Part II: Write the meaning of these words.

Example: unsealed _____ not sealed _____

1. unimportant _____

2. unseen _____

3. unprepared _____

4. unwritten _____

5. unread _____

6. unsafe _____

7. unlit _____

8. uninterested _____

9. unsold _____

10. uncommon _____

untied

untied

untied

untied

More Practice with the Prefix *un-*

The prefix *un-* means "not."

uneaten	unusual	untie	unknown	unhappy	unused
unable	unsure	undid	unspoken	uncover	unclean

Part I: Choose the word from the box above that best completes each sentence and write it on the line. Each word is used once.

1. Please _____ the baby's shoes and remove them.

2. The sobbing little boy looked very _____.

3. The man was _____ to get to work on time.

4. The color of that fabric is very _____.

5. The blank paper in this box appears to be _____.

6. It took a long time to carefully _____ the fossils.

7. The family had an _____ rule about tickling.

8. He _____ the latch and opened the gate.

9. Since Sherry was _____ what to do, she didn't do anything.

10. No one knows the name of the man who lies in the Tomb of the _____ Soldier.

11. I didn't want to drink from the glass because it looked _____.

12. The family left so quickly that their _____ dinner still sat on the table.

Part II: Pick two words from the box at the top of the page. Use each word in a sentence.

Example: I was **unable** to reach the phone before it stopped ringing.

1. _____

_____

2. _____

_____

The Prefix *pre-*

When the prefix *pre-* starts a word, it means "before."

Examples: *prepaid* means "paid before"

preorder means "order before"

Part I: Form words by adding *pre* to the base word. Write the word on the line.

Example: view before _____preview_____

1. heat before _____

2. caution before _____

3. test before _____

4. recorded before _____

5. set before _____

6. wash before _____

Part II: Match the word to its meaning. Write the letter on the line next to the word.

1. _____ prepare

2. _____ prepay

3. _____ preheat

4. _____ preschool

5. _____ preset

6. _____ prefix

7. _____ pretest

8. _____ precaution

9. _____ prehistoric

10. _____ predict

a. heat before

b. test before

c. get ready before

d. say something will happen before it does

e. comes at the start of a word

f. pay before

g. before history was written down

h. before kindergarten

i. caution (steps) taken to keep problems from happening

j. set before

prehistoric

prehistoric

prehistoric

prehistoric

More Practice with the Prefix *pre-*

The prefix *pre-* means "before."

prepare	prepay	preheat	preschool	preset	preview
pretest	prefix	precaution	prehistoric	predict	preface

Part I: Choose the word from the box above that best completes each sentence and write it on the line. Each word is used once.

1. The word-processing program had _____ margins.

2. A _____ comes before the main part of a book.

3. As a _____, Dad covered the windows before the hurricane.

4. Before kindergarten, I went to _____ for two years.

5. If you give Sam the recipe, I'm sure he will _____ the dish.

6. Before baking, you must first _____ the oven to 375°F.

7. Dinosaurs are _____ animals.

8. Anna scored an 85 on the math _____ for addition.

9. If you _____ for your tickets, you'll save $10.

10. The letters "pre" form a _____ that means "before."

11. The weather forecast did not _____ the heavy rain.

12. The movie's _____ made it look exciting.

Part II: Pick two words from the box at the top of the page. Use each word in a sentence.

Example: ___Let's **prepare** our lunches for tomorrow.___

1. _____

   _____

2. _____

   _____

The Prefix *re-*

When the prefix *re-* starts a word, it means "again."

Examples: *restart* means "start again"

reorder means "order again"

Part I: Form words by adding *re* to the base word. Write the word on the line.

Example: heated again _____reheated_____

1. gain again_____
2. done again _____
3. test again _____
4. count again_____
5. enter again _____
6. load again_____

7. organize again _____
8. set again _____
9. claim again_____
10. run again _____
11. wound again_____
12. submit again_____

Part II: Write the meaning of these words.

Example: redesign _____design again_____

1. redecorate _____
2. review _____
3. replay _____
4. repaint _____
5. reappear _____

6. recall_____
7. rewind _____
8. rearrange _____
9. redo _____
10. rewrite _____

rewrite

rewrite

rewrite

rewrite

More Practice with the Prefix *re-*

The prefix *re-* means "again."

reviewed	replay	rebuilt	rewrite	reappear	repaint
remember	recharged	rewind	reentry	replace	rearrange

Part I: Choose the word from the box that best completes each sentence and write it on the line. Each word is used once.

1. Did you _____ to do your homework?

2. Let's help Ben _____ the furniture in his room.

3. After the teacher _____ my test, he smiled and said I'd earned a good grade.

4. Be sure to get your hand stamped for _____ to the amusement park.

5. My mom wants to _____ this room a different shade of green.

6. Did Sarah _____ the vase that she broke?

7. Please _____ this video tape to the beginning.

8. The shed had caved in, so it had to be _____.

9. Suddenly the dog seemed to _____ out of nowhere.

10. We watched the instant _____ of the football fumble.

11. To get a better grade, you may need to _____ your report.

12. That battery has run down and needs to be _____.

Part II: Pick two words from the box at the top of the page. Use each word in a sentence.

Example: Zoe will **rearrange** the flowers in the vase.

1. _____

_____

2. _____

_____

The Prefix *dis-*

When the prefix *dis-* starts a word, it means "opposite." Many words beginning with *dis-* are negative words.

   Examples: *discourage* means "the opposite of encourage"

                discontinue means "the opposite of continue"

Part I: Form words by adding *dis* to the base word. Write the word on the line.

   Example: opposite of allowed   disallowed

1. opposite of trust _____

2. opposite of covered _____

3. opposite of loyal _____

4. opposite of regard _____

5. opposite of courteous _____

6. opposite of belief _____

7. opposite of mount _____

8. opposite of honor _____

9. opposite of interest _____

10. opposite of obeyed _____

Part II: An *antonym* is a word that means the opposite of another. *Big* and *little* are antonyms.

disagree	dissatisfied	disappear	disbelief	disable	discourage
disgrace	dishonest	dislike	disobey	displeased	disallow

Choose an antonym from the box above and write it on the line provided.

   Example: trust   distrust

1. like _____

2. grace _____

3. honest _____

4. allow _____

5. belief _____

6. satisfied _____

7. obey _____

8. appear _____

9. pleased _____

10. able _____

11. agree _____

12. encourage _____

More Practice with the Prefix *dis-*

The prefix *dis-* means "opposite." Words beginning with *dis-* often have negative meanings.

disagree	disabled	disappear	disbelief	discover	discouraged
disgrace	dishonest	disliked	disinfect	displeased	disrepair

Part I: Choose the word from the box above that best completes each sentence and write it on the line. Each word is used once.

1. Robert immediately _____ the growling dog.

2. The nurse will _____ the cut and then bandage it.

3. I _____ with your idea.

4. The _____ woman sat in a wheelchair.

5. The old house had fallen into _____.

6. Did Christopher Columbus _____ America?

7. People who lie are called _____.

8. The teacher told me not to be _____ by my poor grade.

9. I hoped that the bunny wouldn't go back into the woods and _____ from sight.

10. Joshua stared at the girl with shock and _____.

11. It's a _____ to throw food wrappers and soda cans on the ground.

12. If you are _____ with the item, you can return it for a refund.

Part II: Pick two words from the box at the top of the page. Use each word in a sentence.

Example: I was pleased to **discover** a $5 bill in my pocket.

1. _____

   _____

2. _____

   _____

The Prefix *out-*

When the prefix *out-* starts a word, it means "beyond."

   Examples: *outlying* area means "the area lying beyond"

   outward means "to go beyond where you are; move beyond"

Part I: Match the word to its meaning. Write the letter on the line next to the word.

1. _____ outbid

2. _____ outran

3. _____ outsell

4. _____ outlaw

5. _____ outnumber

6. _____ outdoors

7. _____ outspoken

8. _____ outgoing

9. _____ outdo

10. _____ outboard

a. beyond doors; not inside

b. do beyond what was expected

c. going beyond to be friendly to others

d. to bid higher than someone else bid

e. to sell more than another

f. a number beyond another

g. a motor that's beyond (outside of) a boat

h. to speak beyond what most people would say

i. a person who does something against (beyond) the law

j. ran farther or faster than someone else

Part II: Read the sentence. Think about what the **bolded** word means. Then circle the letter of the correct answer.

1. If Cam can **outlast** the others, he'll win the contest. *Outlast* means

   (a) to not last as long.

   (b) to last longer.

   (c) to tie with.

   (d) to laugh at.

2. Ella **outweighs** Madison by 12 pounds. *Outweighs* means

   (a) to weigh more.

   (b) to weigh the same.

   (c) to weigh less.

   (d) to not know one's weight.

3. Have you already **outgrown** that shirt? *Outgrown* means

   (a) stained.

   (b) torn.

   (c) grown beyond.

   (d) grown smaller.

outgrown

More Practice with the Prefix *out-*

The prefix *out-* means "beyond."

outgrew	outbid	outdone	outstanding	outlived	outlaw
outnumber	outran	outboard	outgoing	outdoors	outspoken

Part I: Choose the word from the box that best completes each sentence and write it on the line. Each word is used once.

1. The pairs of pants Betsy owns _____ her dresses.

2. If Shane gets _____ during the auction, he won't get the item.

3. You've _____ everyone else with these holiday decorations!

4. He _____ the rest of the runners and won the race.

5. The woman _____ her husband by six years.

6. Mrs. Durant is very _____ about the amount of pollution in the lake.

7. The _____ hoped the policewoman couldn't see him.

8. Joey _____ this pair of jeans in just one month!

9. The boat's _____ motor quit working.

10. You deserved the _____ grade you got on that report.

11. The new student is so _____ that she'll soon have plenty of friends.

12. It's such a beautiful day that we should spend it _____.

Part II: Pick two words from the box at the top of the page. Use each word in a sentence.

Example: Jody is an **outstanding** singer.

1. _____

_____

2. _____

_____

The Prefix *sub-*

When the prefix *sub-* starts a word, it means "below" or "down."

Examples: *subside* means "to go down; decrease"

subheading means "a heading below; of less importance than the main heading"

Part I: Form words by adding *sub* to the base word. Write the word on the line:

Example: urban _____suburban_____

1. way _____

2. heading _____

3. standard _____

4. set _____

5. title _____

6. merge _____

7. marine _____

8. soil_____

Part II: Match the word to its meaning. Write the letter on the line next to the word.

____ 1. sub-zero

____ 2. substitute

____ 3. subsoil

____ 4. submerge

____ 5. subtitle

____ 6. submarine

____ 7. subset

____ 8. suburb

____ 9. subtracting

____ 10. subside

a. a person or thing that takes the place of another

b. a ship that moves underwater; under the sea

c. decrease; become less

d. below freezing temperature (on the Fahrenheit scale)

e. a layer of dirt beneath the topsoil

f. a smaller part of a larger group

g. go below

h. taking away

i. title (words) below a picture or other words

j. the area outside of an urban area (city)

submarine

submarine

More Practice with the Prefix *Sub-*

The prefix *sub* means "below" or "down."

subway	submarine	substandard	sub-zero	subsoil	substitute
subtitle	submerged	subtract	subset	suburbs	subsided

Part I: Choose the word from the box that best completes each sentence and write it on the line. Each word is used once.

1. The _____ smoothly slid below the water's surface.

2. The _____ temperature makes it hard to stay outdoors.

3. When a book has a main title and a secondary title, the second one is a _____.

4. Mrs. Barrens was absent today, so we had a _____ teacher.

5. The numbers 2, 4, 6, and 8 are a _____ of the set of all even numbers.

6. When a math equation has a minus sign, you must _____ the numbers.

7. They live outside of the city in the _____.

8. The log was partly _____ in the swamp.

9. This house is falling apart because it was built with _____ materials.

10. We had to dig down about three feet into the _____ to reach the treasure box.

11. After her fever _____, Tracy felt much better.

12. Mel rode the _____ all the way from Fifth Avenue to 61st Street.

Part II: Pick two words from the box at the top of the page. Use each word in a sentence.

Example: _When you **subtract**, you get a smaller number._

1. _____

_____

2. _____

_____

The Prefix *under-*

When the prefix *under-* starts a word, it means "under" or "not enough."

Examples: *underside* means "the side under; bottom"

underline means "draw a line under"

Part I: Form words by adding under to the base word. Write the word on the line:

Example: stand _____understand_____

1. tow _____

2. cover _____

3. score _____

4. brush _____

5. study _____

6. shirt _____

7. dressed _____

8. ground _____

9. pants _____

10. went _____

Part II: Write the meaning of these words.

Example: underfed _____not fed enough_____

1. underwater _____

2. underarm _____

3. underfoot _____

4. underpaid _____

5. underpriced _____

6. underneath _____

7. underlying _____

8. undercurrent _____

undercover

undercover

undercover

undercover

More Practice with the Prefix *under-*

The prefix *under-* means "under" or "not enough."

understood	undercover	underlying	underbrush	underline	underweight
underpaid	undershirt	undertow	underdressed	underneath	underwater

Part I: Choose the word from the box above that best completes each sentence and write it on the line. Each word is used once.

1. At the fancy restaurant, I felt very _____ in my jeans.

2. Stacy's work is easily worth $10 per hour, but she is _____ at $7 per hour.

3. The juice soaked through his dress shirt and stained his _____ , too.

4. Please _____ the name of the recipe you'd like to borrow from this list.

5. I'm not sure that I _____ what Ryan meant.

6. Studying animals that live _____ has always interested Matt.

7. No one swims there due to the strong _____, which can pull people under.

8. We pushed aside the _____ and went deeper into the forest.

9. The doctor said that Shannon was _____ and needed to gain about 10 pounds.

10. The _____ police officer was on a stake-out near the mall.

11. The money is hidden in a box she keeps _____ her bed.

12. The _____ problem is a lack of time.

Part II: Pick two words from the box at the top of the page. Use each word in a sentence.

Example: I found the tickets **underneath** a stack of papers.

1. _____

_____

2. _____

_____

The Suffixes *-s* and *-es* for Plurals

The suffix *-s* at the end of nouns shows more than one (plural).

Example: *dogs* means "more than one dog"

Part I: Fill in the chart with words and pictures:

Word for One	Draw One	Word for Two or More	Draw Two
Ex.: monkey		monkeys	
1. tree			
2. boy			
3. zebra			
4. book			
5. ski			
6. radio			

When the noun ends in a consonant + *y*, change the *y* to an *i* and add *es* to show more than one (plural).

Example: *cities* means "more than one city."

Part II: Fill in the chart with words and pictures.

Word for One	Draw One	Word for Two or More	Draw Two
Ex.: penny		pennies	
1. candy			
2. body			
3. fly			
4. cherry			

The Suffix *-es* for Plurals

When the suffix *-es* comes at the end of a noun, it means "more than one." For example, *scratches* means "more than one scratch" and *boxes* means "more than one box."

- When a noun ends in *ch, s, sh, x,* or *z,* add *es* to show more than one (plural).
- When a noun ends in a consonant + *o,* add *es* to show more than one (plural).

Part I: Fill in the chart with words and pictures:

Word for One	Draw One	Word for Two or More	Draw Two
Ex.: mosquito		mosquitoes	
1. dish			
2. sandwich			
3. bus			
4. fox			
5. tomato			
6. bush			
7. ax			

Part II: When a noun ends in *f* or *fe*, the *f* often is changed to a *v* before adding *es*.*

Example: two knife _____knives_____

1. five wife _____
2. four hoof _____
3. several elf _____
4. yourself _____
5. nine shelf _____
6. many life _____
7. both wolf _____
8. a few leaf _____

* There are some exceptions to this rule; for example, *staffs* and bank *safes*.

The Suffixes *-d* and *-ed*

The suffixes *-d* and *-ed* show a completed action. When a verb (action word) ends in an *e*, simply add a *d* to show the action is completed. All other verbs use *ed* to show completed action.

Examples: *changed* means "change in the past" (change ends in *e*, so add *d*)

showed means "show in the past" (show ends in a letter other than *e*, so add *ed*)

Part I: Add *-d* or *-ed* to these verbs to show completed action.

Examples: race _____raced_____

walk _____walked_____

1. act _____

2. play _____

3. reach _____

4. live _____

5. miss _____

6. paste _____

7. turn _____

8. chase _____

9. wave _____

10. growl _____

11. hope _____

12. grade _____

Part II: Write the 12 verbs you wrote above on the correct box below. The first one has been done for you.

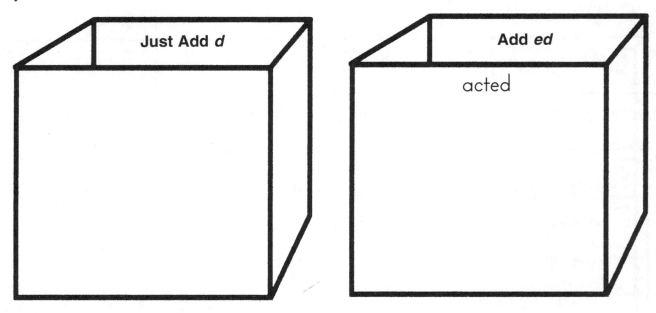

Just Add *d*

Add *ed*

acted

More Rules for the Suffix *-ed*

The suffix *-ed* shows a completed action.

- When a verb ends in a vowel + single consonant, double the consonant and add *ed*.
- When a verb ends in consonant + *y*, change the *y* to an *i* and add *ed*.

Examples: *bragged* means "brag in the past" (double the *g* and add *ed*)

emptied means "empty in the past" (change *y* to *i* and add *ed*)

Part I: Change these verbs to show completed action.

Examples: step ___stepped___

try ___tried___

1. grab _____

2. reply _____

3. nod _____

4. marry _____

5. snap _____

6. beg _____

7. hurry _____

8. slip _____

9. sag _____

10. cry _____

11. deny _____

12. carry _____

Part II: Write the 12 verbs you wrote above on one of these shelves.

Change *y* to *i* and Add *ed*	Double the Consonant and Add *ed*

The Suffixes *-n* and *-en*

The suffixes *-n* and *-en* show completed action for unusual verb forms.

Examples: grown means "grow in the past"

taken means "take in the past"

Part I: Draw a line to match the unusual verb to its completed action form.

1. choose	forgotten		9. break	fallen
2. hide	thrown		10. loose	gotten
3. give	chosen		11. mistake	known
4. forget	hidden		12. beat	mistaken
5. speak	driven		13. know	loosen
6. throw	written		14. fall	beaten
7. drive	given		15. got	broken
8. write	spoken			

Part II: Write these words in A–Z order. The first word has been written for you.

Word	A-Z Order
1. forgotten	beaten
2. known	
3. chosen	
4. mistaken	
5. beaten	
6. broken	
7 given	
8. spoken	
9. fallen	
10. gotten	
11. thrown	
12. hidden	
13. loosen	
14. driven	
15. written	

More Practice with Completed-Action Suffixes

Part I: The completed-action form of each of these verbs ends with the letters *n* or *d*. Write the completed action form for each verb on the lines below.

1.   stop   kiss   shop   rise

     stopped   _____   _____   _____

2.   steal   marry   take   flip

     _____   _____   _____   _____

3.   chase   glide   worry   reach

     _____   _____   _____   _____

Part II: Choose the completed action verb from **Part I** that best completes each sentence. Write it on the line. Each word is used once.

1. My mom _____ that I was lost in the dark.

2. The sun has always _____ in the east.

3. The girl gracefully _____ across the ice.

4. I _____ my grandmother goodbye.

5. After two days the police found the _____ car.

6. The cook _____ over the pancakes.

7. We _____ for six hours and bought a lot of gifts.

8. That dog _____ my cat across the yard.

9. The truck _____ at the red light.

10. My parents got _____ ten years ago.

11. I _____ up to the top shelf to get the can of soup.

12. Have you _____ your medicine yet?

          #8607 PMP: Prefixes & Suffixes Grade 3

The Suffix *-ing*

The suffix *-ing* shows continuous action. Verbs end in *-ing* to show the action is continuing.

One-syllable verbs that end in *ie* change to *y* before adding *ing*.

Examples: *learning* means "continuing to learn"

tying means "continuing to tie"

Part I: Add the suffix *-ing* to these verbs to make the continuous action form of the verb.

Examples: buy _____buying_____

lie _____lying_____

1. join _____
2. say _____
3. spill _____
4. jump _____
5. kick _____
6. die _____
7. sweep _____
8. spy _____

9. display _____
10. start _____
11. tell _____
12. walk _____
13. cry _____
14. stay _____
15. tie _____
16. keep _____

Part II: Read each sentence. Think about the action that's happening. Then darken the circle next to the correct answer.

1. Tamara keeps _____ her bug bite.
   - (a) reaching
   - (b) scratching
   - (c) looking

2. Bill is _____ his dinner early today.
   - (a) eating
   - (b) being
   - (c) keeping

3. The child was _____ about her lost doll.
   - (a) kicking
   - (b) weeping
   - (c) cleaning

More Rules for the Suffix *-ing*

The suffix *-ing* shows continuous action.

- For verbs ending in *e*, drop the *e* and add *-ing* to show continuous action.
- For verbs ending in a vowel + consonant, double the consonant and add *-ing*.

Examples: chasing means "continuing to chase" (drop *e* and add *-ing*)

sipping means "continuing to sip" (double the *p* and add *-ing*)

Part I: Change each of these verbs to its continuous action form by adding *-ing*. Be sure to follow the rules for adding *-ing*.

Examples: hope _____hoping_____

hop _____hopping_____

1. trim _____
2. freeze _____
3. shake _____
4. run _____
5. take _____
6. skip _____
7. shave _____

8. give _____
9. sit _____
10. swim _____
11. wipe _____
12. smile _____
13. cut _____
14. win _____

Part II: Write each of the 14 verbs you wrote above on the correct barrel. The first one has been done for you.

Drop *e* and Add *ing*

Double Consonsant and Add *ing*

trimming

The Suffixes -r and -er

The suffixes *-r* or *-er* are added to an adjective in order to compare two things.

- Add *er* to many adjectives.
- Add *r* to adjectives that end in *e*.

Examples: sweeter means "more sweet than the other"

nicer means "more nice than the other"

Part I: Add *-r* or *-er* to the adjectives to show that two things are being compared.

Examples: high _____ higher _____

large _____ larger _____

1. old _____

2. bright _____

3. close _____

4. late _____

5. low _____

6. white _____

7. slow _____

8. cute _____

9. wide _____

10. dark _____

11. young _____

12. tame _____

Part II: Change the **boldface** word so that it shows a comparison between two things.

Example: Your marker is **new**. _____ Your marker is **newer** than mine. _____

1. My brother is **small**.   My brother is _____ than yours.

2. The brown rabbit acts **tame**.   The brown rabbit acts _____ than the gray one.

3. This color is **bold**.   This color is _____ than that one.

4. Clay came **late** to the party.   Clay came _____ to the party than Joe did.

5. Rachel's voice is **soft**.   Rachel's voice is _____ than Hayley's.

6. This math problem is **hard.**   This math problem is _____ than the other one.

More Rules for the Suffix -er

The suffix -er is added to an adjective in order to compare two things.

- When a word ends in a vowel + consonant, double the consonant and add er.
- When a word ends in a y, change the y to an i and then add er.

Examples: wetter means "more wet than the other"

uglier means "more ugly than the other"

Part I: Add -er to the adjectives to show that two things are being compared. Follow the rules for adding -er.

Examples: sad _____ sadder _____

pretty _____ prettier _____

1. curly _____
2. sad _____
3. dry _____
4. red _____
5. sunny _____
6. heavy _____

7. hot _____
8. early _____
9. funny _____
10. flat _____
11. big _____
12. angry _____

Part II: Change the **boldface** word so that it shows a comparison between two things.

Example: This bush is pretty. This bush is **prettier** than the other one.

1. I am **hungry**.   I am _____ today than I was yesterday.

2. His feet are **big**.   His feet are _____ than mine.

3. Her joke is **funny**.   Her joke is _____ than his.

4. That dress is **ugly**.   That dress is _____ than the first one you wore.

5. This pig is **fat**.   This pig is _____ than the one over there.

6. That towel is **wet**.   That towel is _____ than this one.

7. This box is **heavy**.   This box is _____ than the last one.

The Suffixes -*st* and -*est*

The suffixes -*st* or -*est* are added to an adjective in order to compare more than two things.

- Add *est* to many words.
- Add *st* to words that end in *e*.

Examples: *youngest* means "more young than the others"

latest means "more late than the others"

Part I: Add -*st* or -*est* to these words to show that more than two things are being compared.

Examples: soft _____*softest*_____

blue _____*bluest*_____

1. nice _____

2. cold _____

3. wise _____

4. long _____

5. poor _____

6. close _____

7. rich _____

8. large _____

9. light _____

10. warm _____

11. fierce _____

12. sore _____

Part II: Change the **boldface** word so that it shows comparing more than two.

Example: We were **sick** with the flu. ____When we had the flu, Jim was the____ ____**sickest** of us all.____

1. This crayon is **dull**.

This crayon is the _____ one in the box.

2. This silk is **fine**.

This silk is the _____ I've ever seen.

3. This sweater is **warm**.

This sweater is the _____ of all her sweaters.

4. Pam was **pale**.

Pam was the _____ of the three sisters.

5. The family is **poor**.

The family is the _____ of those we know.

6. The dragon was **fierce**.

The dragon was the _____ one in the forest.

7. That man was **rude**.

That man was the _____ person they'd ever met.

More Rules for the Suffix *-est*

The suffix *-est* is added to a word to compare more than two things.

- When a word ends in a vowel + consonant, double the consonant and add *est*.
- When a word ends in a *y*, change the *y* to an *i* and then add *est*.

Examples: biggest means "more big than the others"

         driest means "more dry than the others"

Part I: Add *-est* to these words to show that more than two things are being compared.

Examples: lazy   laziest

           slim   slimmest

1. sloppy _____

2. sad _____

3. scary _____

4. fat _____

5. sorry _____

6. windy _____

7. tiny _____

8. red _____

9. friendly _____

10. salty _____

11. flat _____

12. hot _____

Part II: Change the boldface word so that it shows comparing more than two.

Example: This test is **easy**.   This test is the **easiest** one we've had so far.

1. That picture is **silly**.   That's the _____ picture you've ever drawn!

2. He had an **unhappy** day.   He had the _____ day of his entire life.

3. My bedroom is **big**.   My bedroom is the _____ of the three in our house.

4. There's a **fat** teddy bear.   There's the _____ teddy bear on the shelf.

5. The dog was **noisy**.   The dog was the _____ one on the block.

6. She is **sad**.   She is the _____ girl I know.

More Practice with Comparative Suffixes

Here is a review:

- Adding the suffixes -r or -er shows comparing two.
- Adding the suffixes -st or -est shows comparing more than two.

Part I: Complete the chart:

Adjective	Adjective Comparing Two	Adjective Comparing More Than Two
Ex.: happy	happier	happiest
1. small		
2. loose		
3. harsh		
4. dim		
5. bold		
6. little		
7. sleepy		
8. thin		
9. saggy		
10. wise		
11. deep		
12. scary		

Part II: Choose the word from the second or third column of **Part I** that best completes each sentence. Not all of the words will be used.

Example: The river's _____ deepest _____ spot is about halfway across.

1. As the light grew _____ , I found it harder to see the trail markers.

2. Since Cody likes short books, he chose the _____ one of the pair.

3. Those pants are so baggy that they're the _____ pair you've tried on so far.

4. As the time for his nap drew near, the child became _____ .

5. Shawn's Frankenstein costume was the _____ one he'd ever worn.

6. Her toy boat is _____ than mine.

7. Mr. Gonzalez is the _____ man I know; he knows something about everything!

8. Ben's punishment was _____ than Ahmed's.

The Suffix -y

The suffix -y means "having the quality of." The suffix -y added to a noun or a verb forms an adjective (describing word).

- If the word ends in a consonant + e, drop the e and add the y.
- When the word ends in a vowel + consonant, double the consonant and add the y.

Examples: wealthy means "having the quality of wealth"

spicy means "having the quality of spice" (drop the e and add the y)

bratty means "having the quality of a brat" (double the consonant and add the y)

Part I: Change these words to adjectives by adding the suffix -y. Follow the rules for adding the suffix.

Examples: luck _____lucky_____

taste _____tasty_____

sun _____sunny_____

1. rain _____
2. weep _____
3. skin _____
4. smoke _____
5. fog _____
6. wave _____

7. ease _____
8. lump _____
9. grease _____
10. health _____
11. slime _____
12. fun _____

Part II: Write these words in A–Z order. The first one has been done for you.

Word	A–Z Order
1. rainy	easy
2. weepy	
3. skinny	
4. smoky	
5. foggy	
6. wavy	
7. easy	
8. lumpy	
9. greasy	
10. healthy	
11. slimy	
12. funny	

More Practice with the Suffix -y

The suffix *-y* means "having the quality of." This suffix turns nouns and verbs into adjectives.

rainy	grimy	smoky	curly	sleepy	breezy
salty	runny	clammy	shiny	bumpy	hasty

Part I: Choose the word from the box above that best completes each sentence and write it on the line. Each word is used once.

1. The pudding didn't set right; it was very_____.

2. It was so _____ that their tent blew over.

3. The brand new car's paint was very _____.

4. Due to the _____ weather, our picnic was cancelled.

5. The _____ air made him cough.

6. I couldn't see in the _____ mirror, so I used my sleeve to rub a clear spot.

7. It's better to take your time than to be _____ in finishing your test.

8. The _____ baby dozed in her father's arms.

9. The ocean's _____ spray smelled good.

10. It was hard to write on such a _____ surface.

11. The little girl's _____ hair was done up with ribbons.

12. When my hand touched something that felt cold and _____, I screamed.

Part II: Pick two words from the box at the top of the page. Use each word in a sentence.

Example: _I felt so **sleepy** I could hardly keep my eyes open._

1. _____

_____

2. _____

_____

The Suffix -ly

When a word ends with the suffix *-ly*, it is usually an adverb. An adverb describes an action. It can also describe an adjective (describing word).

Examples: It was raining *heavily*. (The adverb *heavily* describes how it was raining.)

The baby was *especially* beautiful. (The adverb *especially* describes the adjective *beautiful*, which describes the baby.)

Part I: Form words by adding *-ly* at the end of the base word.

Examples: soft _____softly_____

noise* _____noisily_____

1. loud _____

2. steady* _____

3. slow _____

4. complete _____

5. quiet _____

6. lazy* _____

7. nice _____

8. rapid _____

9. happy* _____

10. cold _____

11. perfect _____

12. hungry* _____

*When the base word ends in *y*, change it to *i* and then add the *ly*.

A *synonym* is a word that means the same thing as another word. *Large* and *big* are synonyms.

Part II: Draw a line to match the adverbs that are synonyms. You may use a thesaurus.

1. | quickly | | fortunately |

2. | sadly | | unexpectedly |

3. | luckily | | rapidly |

4. | steadily | | constantly |

5. | suddenly | | unhappily |

More Practice with the Suffix -ly

Words that end with the suffix -ly are often adverbs. They describe verbs or adjectives.

wearily	possibly	friendly	cuddly	fondly	quietly
merrily	loudly	wisely	totally	suddenly	ghostly

Part I: Choose the word from the box above that best completes each sentence and write it on the line. Each word is used once.

1. It startled me when a man _____ stepped out from the shadows.

2. I can't _____ get there in less than two hours.

3. The boys stared in shock as a _____ image appeared on the screen.

4. The tired little boy _____ sank onto his bed.

5. Hannah _____ tiptoed down the hall.

6. Did $10 _____ cover the bill?

7. The car's brakes squealed _____.

8. Jon _____ decided not to say anything rude.

9. All of the kids laughed _____ when they heard her jokes.

10. The father smiled _____ at his newborn baby.

11. The teddy bear looked cute and _____.

12. Everyone likes Michelle because she's so _____.

Part II: Pick two words from the box at the top of the page. Use each word in a sentence.

Example: I greeted my aunt **fondly**.

1. _____

_____

2. _____

_____

The Suffix *-ful*

When a word ends with the suffix *-ful*, it means "full of."

Examples: *thoughtful* means "full of thought"

sinful means "full of sin"

Part I: Write the meaning of these words.

Example: hopeful ___full of hope___

1. beautiful _____
2. playful _____
3. peaceful _____
4. stressful _____

5. useful _____
6. careful _____
7. plentiful _____
8. hateful _____

A *synonym* is a word that means the same thing as another word. *Large* and *big* are synonyms.

sorrowful	peaceful	doubtful	plentiful	cheerful	~~joyful~~
wonderful	grateful	fearful	faithful	thoughtful	

Part II: Choose a synonym from the box above and write it in the second column. You may use a thesaurus.

Word	Synonym
Example: glad	joyful
1. uncertain	
2. calm	
3. terrific	
4. abundant	
5. loyal	
6. thankful	
7. sad	
8. happy	
9. caring	
10. afraid	

More Practice with the Suffix *-ful*

The suffix *-ful* means "full of."

careful	stressful	joyful	faithful	harmful	beautiful
hopeful	wasteful	helpful	painful	cheerful	doubtful

Part I: Choose the word from the box that best completes each sentence and write it on the line. Each word is used once.

1. Ashley was _____ not to knock the dish off the table.

2. Having three tests in one day was very _____ for me.

3. Tom's headache was _____ but only lasted a few hours.

4. Smoking is _____ to a person's health.

5. The doctor was so _____ that she made her patients smile.

6. It's _____ that it will snow on such a warm day.

7. Throwing out good food is _____.

8. When we had a flat tire, a _____ man changed it for us.

9. Alyssa was _____ and kept her promise to me.

10. Abraham feels _____ that he will get six gifts on his birthday.

11. The actress had _____ long blonde hair.

12. People call the holidays a _____ season.

Part II: Pick two words from the box at the top of the page. Use each word in a sentence.

Example: _____ When I broke my arm, it was **painful**.

1. _____

_____

2. _____

_____

The Suffix -less

When a word ends with the suffix -less, it means "without."

Examples: harmless means "without harm"

endless means "without end"

Part I: Write the meaning of these words.

Example: without hope ___hopeless___

1. without time _____

2. without need _____

3. without age _____

4. without regard _____

5. without taste _____

6. without shame _____

7. without help _____

8. without joy _____

9. without heart _____

10. without hair _____

11. without humor _____

12. without worth _____

An *antonym* is a word that means the opposite of another word. Words that end in -less and -ful are often antonyms to each other.

Part II: Write the antonym of the word given. The words will end in -less or -ful.

Example: tactful ___tactless___

#			
1.	thankful	→	
2.		→	fearless
3.	careful	→	
4.		→	painless
5.	meaningful	→	
6.		→	useless
7.	thoughtful	→	
8.		→	hopeless
9.	harmful	→	
10.		→	doubtless

More Practice with the Suffix *-less*

The suffix *-less* means "without."

careless	worthless	hopeless	helpless	tasteless	homeless
fearless	sleepless	useless	thoughtless	harmless	tireless

Part I: Choose the word from the box above that best completes each sentence and write it on the line. Each word is used once.

1. Due to the doctor's _____ efforts, the sick child was cured.

2. The _____ boy rode his bike off the ramp.

3. A butter knife is _____ for slicing ham.

4. It was _____ of me to be so rude to you.

5. The money wasn't real, so it was _____.

6. She runs a shelter where _____ people can sleep.

7. Because someone was _____ with a campfire, many trees in the forest burned.

8. Once Ken was tied up with ropes, he was completely_____ .

9. After a _____ night, Zayne was very tired.

10. These brownies are _____!

11. Since her cat hadn't been seen for ten days, Alison feared her search was _____.

12. Although the dog growled, she was _____.

Part II: Pick two words from the box at the top of the page. Use each word in a sentence.

Example: _A homeless family lived under the bridge._

1. _____

_____

2. _____

_____

The Suffix *-ish*

The suffix *-ish* means "relating to." Adding *-ish* to a noun changes it to an adjective. An adjective is a describing word.

Examples: *feverish* means "relating to a fever"

          stylish means "relating to style" (The *e* is dropped at the end before adding the *ish*.)

          Irish means "relating to Ireland" (Only part of *Ireland* is included in the adjective.)

Part I: Match the adjective to its related noun. Write the letter on the line next to the word.

_____ 1. nourish   a. self

_____ 2. childish   b. forty

_____ 3. boyish   c. England

_____ 4. finish   d. furniture

_____ 5. Swedish   e. nutrition

_____ 6. selfish   f. final

_____ 7. foolish   g. red

_____ 8. fortyish   h. boy

_____ 9. reddish   i. Sweden

_____ 10. English   j. fool

_____ 11. ticklish   k. child

_____ 12. furnish   l. tickle

Part II: Form an adjective ending in *-ish* that fits the definition given.

Example: a man in his fifties _____fiftyish_____

1. a person acting like a fool _____

2. someone who comes from Ireland _____

3. complete a project _____

4. buy furniture for a house _____

5. the language spoken in Spain _____

6. relating to the color gray _____

7. an adult who acts like a child _____

8. a person who thinks only about herself _____

More Practice with the Suffix *-ish*

The suffix *-ish* means "relating to."

childish	thirtyish	British	girlish	whitish	Spanish
finish	nourish	unselfish	ticklish	feverish	stylish

Part I: Choose the word from the box that best completes each sentence and write it on the line. Each word is used once.

1. The BBC stands for the _____ Broadcasting Company, located in Great Britain.

2. Brynn is so _____ that she starts to squeal if I even reach out to tickle her.

3. The ill person looked flushed and _____.

4. Katrina had on a _____ dress and a hat with a feather.

5. Many people in South America speak the _____ language.

6. The store clerk pouted in a _____ manner.

7. A _____ powder covered the surface of the box.

8. It is _____ of you to give money to the needy.

9. As the puppy squirmed in her lap, the old lady gave a _____ giggle.

10. After you _____ that project, I have something else for you to do.

11. We need to _____ the children with good food and vitamins.

12. The man, who looked _____, had a beard and glasses.

Part II: Pick two words from the box at the top of the page. Use each word in a sentence.

Example: __It was **unselfish** of my sister to share her candy with me.__

1. _____

_____

2. _____

_____

The Suffix *-ness*

The suffix *-ness* means "state of or quality of." Adding *-ness* to an adjective (describing word) changes it into a noun (thing).

Examples: *fairness* means "the quality of being fair"

darkness means "the state of being dark"

Part I: Form nouns by adding *-ness* at the end of the adjective. Write the word on the line.

Examples: bright _____brightness_____

friendly* _____friendliness_____

1. hopeful _____

2. silly* _____

3. thankful _____

4. hopeless _____

5. empty* _____

6. foolish _____

7. happy* _____

8. selfish _____

9. kind _____

10. good _____

11. sweet _____

12. ugly* _____

* When the base word ends in *y*, change it to *i* and then add the *ness*.

An *antonym* is a word that means the opposite of another word. *Tall* and *short* are antonyms.

Part II: Draw a line to match the words that are antonyms.

1. | hopefulness   hardness

2. | carelessness   thoughtlessness

3. | fullness   niceness

4. | softness   hopelessness

5. | thoughtfulness   carefulness

6. | harshness   emptiness

More Practice with the Suffix *-ness*

The suffix *-ness* means "state or quality of." Adding *-ness* to the end of an adjective turns it into a noun.

illness	kindness	softness	wilderness	darkness	fanciness
unhappiness	coldness	thickness	lateness	roughness	sweetness

Part I: Choose the word from the box that best completes each sentence and write it on the line. Each word is used once.

1. The cake's _____ was a bit too much.

2. It's really hard to take a photo in this _____.

3. Thank you for your _____ in fixing my toy.

4. Kyle's _____ made him have a fever.

5. When he heard that he had two cavities, Michael's _____ showed on his face.

6. The family took a compass so that they wouldn't get lost in the _____.

7. The _____ of Joanna's gown surprised us.

8. A blast of _____ came from the open freezer door.

9. The wooden board's _____ made sitting on it uncomfortable.

10. The folder's _____ meant that it held lots of papers.

11. She reached out and felt the _____ of the doll's skin.

12. I asked the reason for his _____ when he came an hour after my party started.

Part II: Pick two words from the box at the top of the page. Use each word in a sentence.

Example: The **darkness** made it hard to see.

1. _____

_____

2. _____

_____

Assessment 1

Darken the circle of the correct answer.

1. **The word *refill* means**
   - (a) to overfill
   - (b) to fill again
   - (c) to fill more than the other

2. **The word *displeased* means**
   - (a) the opposite of pleased
   - (b) never pleased
   - (c) always pleased

3. **The word *prearrange* means**
   - (a) not arrange
   - (b) to arrange after
   - (c) to arrange before

4. **The word *outsell* means**
   - (a) to sell the same amount
   - (b) to sell more
   - (c) to sell less

5. **The word *subgroup* means**
   - (a) a new group
   - (b) a large group
   - (c) part of a larger group

6. **The word *skis* means**
   - (a) a person that teaches skiing
   - (b) more than one ski
   - (c) more than one sky

7. **The word *undergrowth* means**
   - (a) growing below
   - (b) growing above
   - (c) growing slowly

8. **The verb *punched* shows**
   - (a) future action
   - (b) continuous action
   - (c) completed action

9. **The verb *hidden* shows**
   - (a) completed action
   - (b) future action
   - (c) continuous action

10. **The word *closeness* means**
    - (a) less close than many
    - (b) more close than many
    - (c) the state of being close

11. **The word *handiest* means**
    - (a) the most handy
    - (b) more handy than another
    - (c) less handy than others

12. **The word *funny* means**
    - (a) more than fun
    - (b) less than fun
    - (c) having the quality of fun

13. **The adverb *rudely* means**
    - (a) to be rude again
    - (b) less than rude
    - (c) to do action in a rude way

14. **The word *stylish* means**
    - (a) without style
    - (b) relating to style
    - (c) less than style

15. **The word *thickness* means**
    - (a) the state of being thick
    - (b) too thick
    - (c) more thick than several others

Assessment 2

Darken the circle of the correct answer. Not all of the choices are actual words.

1. **Choose the word that means the opposite of *regard*.**
   - (a) preregard
   - (b) subregard
   - (c) outregard
   - (d) disregard

2. **Choose the word that means "below the soil."**
   - (a) subsoil
   - (b) outsoil
   - (c) dissoil
   - (d) resoil

3. **Choose the word that means "to submit again."**
   - (a) unsubmit
   - (b) resubmit
   - (c) dissubmit
   - (d) presubmit

4. **Choose the word that means "not nourished enough."**
   - (a) subnourished
   - (b) outnourished
   - (c) undernourished
   - (d) renourished

5. **Choose the word that means "lies beyond an area."**
   - (a) underlying area
   - (b) outlying area
   - (c) relying area
   - (d) sublying area

6. **Choose the word that means "recorded before."**
   - (a) prerecorded
   - (b) unrecorded
   - (c) rerecorded
   - (d) subrecorded

7. **Choose the word that means "not paid."**
   - (a) underpaid
   - (b) dispaid
   - (c) prepaid
   - (d) unpaid

8. **Choose the verb that shows a completed action and means "continue in the past."**
   - (a) continues
   - (b) continuing
   - (c) continuen
   - (d) continued

9. **Choose the verb that shows a completed action and means "beat in the past."**
   - (a) beaten
   - (b) beats
   - (c) beated
   - (d) beating

10. **Choose the word that means "more tight than another."**
    - (a) tightful
    - (b) tightly
    - (c) tighter
    - (d) tightest

11. **Choose the word that means "having the quality to scare."**
    - (a) scarely
    - (b) scary
    - (c) scareful
    - (d) scareless

12. **Choose the adverb that means "take action in a rapid way."**
    - (a) rapidly
    - (b) rapidy
    - (c) rapids
    - (d) rapidful

13. **Choose the word that means "without a penny."**
    - (a) pennyish
    - (b) pennily
    - (c) penniless
    - (d) pennyless

14. **Choose the word that means "full of power."**
    - (a) powerful
    - (b) powerless
    - (c) powerly
    - (d) powerish

15. **Choose the word that means "having the quality of being kind."**
    - (a) kindful
    - (b) kindy
    - (c) kinder
    - (d) kindness

Summary of Prefixes and Suffixes

Prefix	Means	Prefix	Means	Suffix	Means	Suffix	Means
un-	not	pre-	before	-s, -es	plural, more than one	-ish	relating to
re-	again	dis-	opposite	-d, -ed	completed action	-ful	full of
out-	beyond	sub-	below, down	-n, -en	completed action	-less	without
		under-	under, not enough	-ing	continuous action (verb)	-ly	adverb, describes action
				-r, -er	comparing two	-ness	state or quality of
		-		-st, -est	comparing more than two	-y	having the quality of

Answer Key

Page 4
Part I
1. unused
2. untied
3. unhappy
4. uncertain
5. unspoken
6. unusual
7. unknown
8. unable
9. undo
10. uncover

Part II
1. not important
2. not seen
3. not prepared
4. not written
5. not read
6. not safe
7. not lit
8. not interested
9. not sold
10. not common

Page 5
Part I
1. untie
2. unhappy
3. unable
4. unusual

5. unused
6 uncover
7. unspoken
8. undid
9. unsure
10. Unknown
11. unclean
12. uneaten

Page 6
Part I
1. preheat
2. precaution
3. pretest
4. prerecorded
5. preset
6. prewash

Part II
1. c   5. j   9. g
2. f   6. e   10. d
3. a   7. b
4. h   8. i

Page 7
1. preset
2. preface
3. precaution
4. preschool
5. prepare
6. preheat
7. prehistoric

8. pretest
9. prepay
10. prefix
11. predict
12. preview

Page 8
Part I
1. regain
2. redone
3. retest
4. recount
5. reenter
6. reload
7. reorganize
8. reset
9. reclaim
10. rerun
11. rewound
12. resubmit

Part II
1. decorate again
2. view again
3. play again
4. paint again
5. appear again
6. call again
7. wind again
8. arrange again
9. do again
10. write again

Page 9
1. remember
2. rearrange
3. reviewed
4. reentry
5. repaint
6. replace
7. rewind
8. rebuilt
9. reappear
10. replay
11. rewrite
12. recharged

Page 10
Part I
1. distrust
2. discovered
3. disloyal
4. disregard
5. discourteous
6. disbelief
7. dismount
8. dishonor
9. disinterest
10. disobeyed

Part II
1. dislike
2. disgrace
3. dishonest
4. disallow

Answer Key *(cont.)*

5. disbelief
6. dissatisfied
7. disobey
8. disappear
9. displeased
10. disable
11. disagree
12. discourage

Page 11
1. disliked
2. disinfect
3. disagree
4. disabled
5. disrepair
6. discover
7. dishonest
8. discouraged
9. disappear
10. disbelief
11. disgrace
12. displeased

Page 12
Part I
1. d
2. j
3. e
4. i
5. f
6. a
7. h
8. c
9. b
10. g

Part II
1. b
2. a
3. c

Page 13
1. outnumber
2. outbid
3. outdone
4. outran
5. outlived
6. outspoken
7. outlaw
8. outgrew
9. outboard
10. outstanding
11. outgoing
12. outdoors

Page 14
Part I
1. subway
2. subheading

3. substandard
4. subset
5. subtitle
6. submerge
7. submarine
8. subsoil

Part II
1. d   6. b
2. a   7. f
3. e   8. j
4. g   9. h
5. i   10. c

Page 15
1. submarine
2. sub-zero
3. subtitle
4. substitute
5. subset
6. subtract
7. suburbs
8. submerged
9. substandard
10. subsoil
11. subsided
12. subway

Page 16
Part I
1. undertow
2. undercover
3. underscore
4. underbrush
5. understudy
6. undershirt
7. underdressed
8. underground
9. underpants
10. underwent

Part II
1. below the water
2. below the arm
3. below the foot
4. not paid enough
5. not priced high enough
6. under something
7. lying under
8. the current under the surface

Page 17
1. underdressed
2. underpaid
3. undershirt
4. underline
5. understood
6. underwater
7. undertow

8. underbrush
9. underweight
10. undercover
11. underneath
12. underlying

Page 18
Part I
1. trees
2. boys
3. zebras
4. books
5. skis
6. radios

Part II
1. candies
2. bodies
3. flies
4. cherries

Page 19
Part I
1. dishes
2. sandwiches
3. buses
4. foxes
5. tomatoes
6. bushes
7. axes

Part II
1. wives
2. hooves
3. elves
4. yourselves
5. shelves
6. lives
7. wolves
8. leaves

Page 20
1. acted
2. played
3. reached
4. lived
5. missed
6. pasted
7. turned
8. chased
9. waved
10. growled
11. hoped
12. graded

Add *d* Box
lived
pasted
chased
waved

hoped
graded

Add *ed* Box
acted
played
reached
missed
turned
growled

Page 21
1. grabbed
2. replied
3. nodded
4. married
5. snapped
6. begged
7. hurried
8. slipped
9. sagged
10. cried
11. denied
12. carried

ied bookshelf:
replied
married
hurried
cried
denied
carried

double consonant, add *ed* bookshelf:
grabbed
nodded
snapped
begged
slipped
sagged

Page 22
Part I
1. choose—chosen
2. hide—hidden
3. give—given
4. forget—forgotten
5. speak—spoken
6. throw—thrown
7. drive—driven
8. write—written
9. break—broken
10. loose—loosen
11. mistake—mistaken
12. beat—beaten
13. know—known
14. fall—fallen
15. got—gotten

Answer Key (cont.)

Part II
1. beaten
2. broken
3. chosen
4. driven
5. fallen
6. forgotten
7. given
8. gotten
9. hidden
10. known
11. loosen
12. mistaken
13. spoken
14. thrown
15. written

Page 23
Part I
1. stopped, kissed, shopped, risen
2. stolen, married, taken, flipped
3. chased, glided, worried, reached

Part II
1. worried
2. risen
3. glided
4. kissed
5. stolen
6. flipped
7. shopped
8. chased
9. stopped
10. married
11. reached
12. taken

Page 24
Part I
1. joining
2. saying
3. spilling
4. jumping
5. kicking
6. dying
7. sweeping
8. spying
9. displaying
10. starting
11. telling
12. walking
13. crying
14. staying
15. tying
16. keeping

Part II
1. b
2. a
3. b

Page 25
1. trimming
2. freezing
3. shaking
4. running
5. taking
6. skipping
7. shaving
8. giving
9. sitting
10. swimming
11. wiping
12. smiling
13. cutting
14. winning

Drop e Barrel:
freezing
shaking
taking
shaving
giving
wiping
smiling

Double Consonant Barrel:
trimming
running
skipping
sitting
swimming
cutting
winning

Page 26
Part I
1. older
2. brighter
3. closer
4. later
5. lower
6. whiter
7. slower
8. cuter
9. wider
10. darker
11. younger
12. tamer

Part II
1. smaller
2. tamer
3. bolder
4. later
5. softer
6. harder

Page 27
Part I
1. curlier
2. sadder
3. drier
4. redder
5. sunnier
6. heavier
7. hotter
8. earlier
9. funnier
10. flatter
11. bigger
12. angrier

Part II
1. hungrier
2. bigger
3. funnier
4. uglier
5. fatter
6. wetter
7. heavier

Page 28
Part I
1. nicest
2. coldest
3. wisest
4. longest
5. poorest
6. closest
7. richest
8. largest
9. lightest
10. warmest
11. fiercest
12. sorest

Part II
1. dullest
2. finest
3. warmest
4. palest
5. poorest
6. fiercest
7. rudest

Page 29
Part I
1. sloppiest
2. saddest
3. scariest
4. fattest
5. sorriest
6. windiest
7. tiniest
8. reddest
9. friendliest
10. saltiest

11. flattest
12. hottest

Part II
1. silliest
2. unhappiest
3. biggest
4. fattest
5. noisiest
6. saddest

Page 30
Part I
1. smaller, smallest
2. looser, loosest
3. harsher, harshest
4. dimmer, dimmest
5. bolder, boldest
6. littler, littlest
7. sleepier, sleepiest
8. thinner, thinnest
9. saggier, saggiest
10. wiser, wisest
11. deeper, deepest
12. scarier, scariest

Part II
1. dimmer
2. thinner
3. loosest, saggiest
4. sleepier
5. scariest
6. smaller, littler
7. wisest
8. harsher

Page 31
Part I
1. rainy
2. weepy
3. skinny
4. smoky
5. foggy
6. wavy
7. easy
8. lumpy
9. greasy
10. healthy
11. slimy
12. funny

Part II
1. easy
2. foggy
3. funny
4. greasy
5. healthy
6. lumpy
7. rainy
8. skinny
9. slimy

Answer Key (cont.)

10. smoky
11. wavy
12. weepy

Page 32
1. runny
2. breezy
3. shiny
4. rainy
5. smoky
6. grimy
7. hasty
8. sleepy
9. salty
10. bumpy
11. curly
12. clammy

Page 33
Part I
1. loudly
2. steadily
3. slowly
4. completely
5. quietly
6. lazily
7. nicely
8. rapidly
9. happily
10. coldly
11. perfectly
12. hungrily

Part II
1. quickly—rapidly
2. sadly—unhappily
3. luckily—fortunately
4. steadily—constantly
5. suddenly—
   unexpectedly

Page 34
1. suddenly
2. possibly
3. ghostly
4. wearily
5. quietly
6. totally
7. loudly
8. wisely
9. merrily
10. fondly
11. cuddly
12. friendly

Page 35
Part I
1. full of beauty
2. full of play

3. full of peace
4. full of stress
5. full of use
6. full of care
7. full of plenty
8. full of hate

Part II
1. doubtful
2. peaceful
3. wonderful
4. plentiful
5. faithful
6. grateful
7. sorrowful
8. cheerful
9. thoughtful
10. fearful

Page 36
1. careful
2. stressful
3. painful
4. harmful
5. cheerful
6. doubtful
7. wasteful
8. helpful
9. faithful
10. hopeful
11. beautiful
12. joyful

Page 37
Part I
1. timeless
2. needless
3. ageless
4. regardless
5. tasteless
6. shameless
7. helpless
8. joyless
9. heartless
10. hairless
11. humorless
12. worthless

Part II
1. thankless
2. fearful
3. careless
4. painful
5. meaningless
6. useful
7. thoughtless
8. hopeful
9. harmless
10. doubtful

Page 38
1. tireless
2. fearless
3. useless
4. thoughtless
5. worthless
6. homeless
7. careless
8. helpless
9. sleepless
10. tasteless
11. hopeless
12. harmless

Page 39
Part I
1. e
2. k
3. h
4. f
5. i
6. a
7. j
8. b
9. g
10. c
11. l
12. d

Part II
1. foolish
2. Irish
3. finish
4. furnish
5. Spanish
6. grayish
7. childish
8. selfish

Page 40
1. British
2. ticklish
3. feverish
4. stylish
5. Spanish
6. childish
7. whitish
8. unselfish
9. girlish
10. finish
11. nourish
12. thirtyish

Page 41
Part I
1. hopefulness
2. silliness
3. thankfulness

4. hopelessness
5. emptiness
6. foolishness
7. happiness
8. selfishness
9. kindness
10. goodness
11. sweetness
12. ugliness

Part II
1. hopefulness—
   hopelessness
2. carelessness—
   carefulness
3. fullness—emptiness
4. softness—hardness
5. thoughtfulness—
   thoughtlessness
6. harshness—niceness

Page 42
1. sweetness
2. darkness
3. kindness
4. illness
5. unhappiness
6. wilderness
7. fanciness
8. coldness
9. roughness
10. thickness
11. softness
12. lateness

Page 43
1. b	9. a
2. a	10. c
3. c	11. a
4. b	12. c
5. c	13. c
6. b	14. b
7. a	15. a
8. c	

Page 44
1. d	9. a
2. a	10. c
3. b	11. b
4. c	12. a
5. b	13. c
6. a	14. a
7. d	15. d
8. d	